D0805459

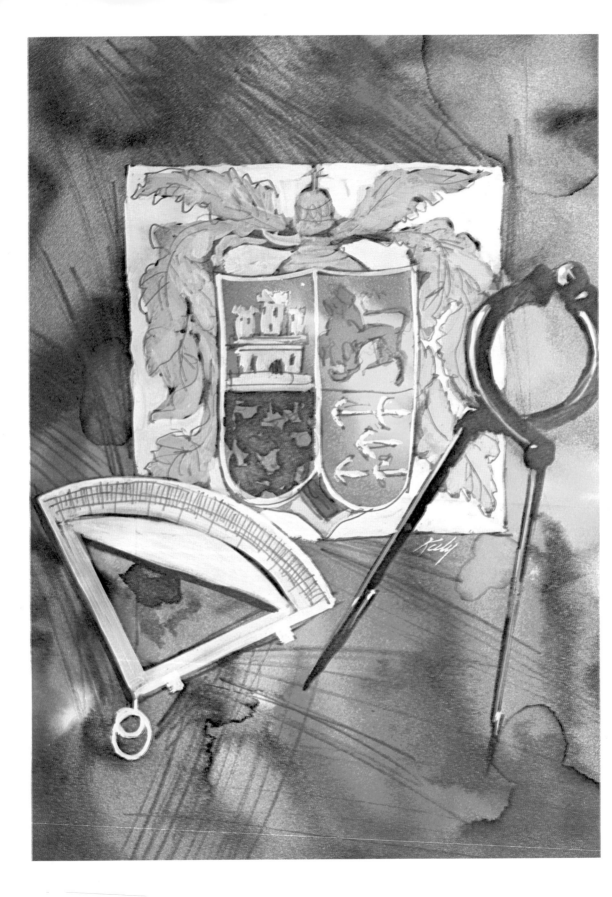

WE
THE PEOPLE
COLUMBUS

Published by Creative Education, Inc. 123 South
Broad Street, Mankato, Minnesota 56001

Copyright © 1988 by Creative Education, Inc.
International copyrights reserved in all countries.
No part of this book may be reproduced in any form
without written permission from the publisher.
Printed in the United States.

Library of Congress Cataloging-in-Publication Data

Zadra, Dan.
  Columbus : discoverer of the New World / Dan Zadra ; illustrated
by John Keely and Dick Brude.

  p. cm. — (We the people)
  Summary: A brief biography of the Italian weaver's son who never
achieved his dream of finding a trade route to India, but in
pursuing it opened the door to the New World.
  ISBN 0-88682-184-3
  1. Columbus, Christopher—Juvenile literature.   2. Explorers—
America—Biography—Juvenile literature.   3. Explorers—Spain—
Biography—Juvenile literature.   4. America—Discovery and
exploration—Spanish—Juvenile literature.   [1. Columbus,
Christopher.   2. Explorers.]   I. Keely, John, ill.   II. Brude,
Dick, ill.   III. Title.   IV. Series: We the people (Mankato, Minn.)
E111.Z23   1988
970.01′5—dc19
[B]   87-36385
[92]   CIP
                                                                                  AC

WE
THE PEOPLE
COLUMBUS

DISCOVERER OF THE NEW WORLD

DAN ZADRA

Illustrated By John Keely and Dick Brude

CENTRAL ARKANSAS LIBRARY SYSTEM
JACKSONVILLE BRANCH
JACKSONVILLE, ARKANSAS

CREATIVE EDUCATION

92 10987

COLUMBUS

Somewhere around the year 1450, a son was born to a poor weaver and his wife in Genoa, Italy. The boy's name was Cristoforo Colombo—Christopher Columbus—and he would grow up to become the man who discovered America.

Christopher's father encouraged his son to become a weaver. But the

boy was fascinated by the great sailing ships that bustled in and out of Genoa's busy harbor. He envied the sailors. "Where are they going, and what do they see?" he wondered. Young Christopher promised himself that he would learn to be a sailor and perhaps have a ship of his own.

Even today, historians aren't quite certain about where and when Christopher went to school. Many believe he may have studied astronomy and navigation at the University of Pavia. We do know that he became an expert seaman and map-maker while still a very young man.

In those days, little was known about the world and its seas. Most Europeans still believed that fire-

breathing serpents roamed the open oceans. It was said that the earth was flat, like an immense table, and that a ship would sail off the edge if it went too far.

At first, Christopher himself believed these stories. But the more he sailed, the more he learned. By 1477, when he was about 27, he had sailed all over the Mediterranean, to England, and perhaps as far as

Iceland. He had never once seen a serpent. "They exist only in the minds of the fearful and superstitious," he would tell his brother Bartolomeo.

More important, a simple experiment convinced Christopher that the earth was round, not flat. Gazing through his telescope, he would watch a ship sail out to sea. "If the earth is flat," he thought, "I should be able to see the ship until it becomes a tiny speck far away on the flat surface." Instead, Christopher saw that the ship disappeared from sight much earlier—as if it had sailed across a curved surface. It was an exciting discovery!

In 1477, Columbus went to live in Portugal where the world's best

sailors were launching important voyages of discovery. There, he married the daughter of Bartholomew Perestrello, a Portugese navigator. Two years later a son, Diego, was born. But Columbus was not a very good father. He was too busy making maps and charts for the Portuguese— or dreaming of distant, uncharted lands.

Around 1482 Columbus hired out as a navigator on a ship bound for the African coast. During the long trip, he had time to think. He was already convinced that the Earth was round. Now he began to wonder if the Earth might not be smaller than most navigators thought. Perhaps the western sea (the Atlantic) was not very wide. Perhaps a ship could cross

it easily—and reach China and Japan by sailing west instead of east!

It was a new, exciting idea. But King John II of Portugal did not think much of it. Columbus asked the king to sponsor a voyage of exploration. "I'll reach the East by sailing West," explained Columbus. But the King just laughed.

Columbus decided to take his idea to Spain. His wife had died, so he took his young son to a monk's school at La Rabida. The kindly prior of the monastery gave Columbus a lettter of introduction to Queen Isabella of Castile.

The year was 1486. Boldly, Columbus strode into Isabella's court. She listened with interest to his plan but was unable to do more

than give him a little money to live on. She and her husband, King Ferdinand, were fighting a war with the Moors.

Five years passed. Columbus met Beatriz Enriquez. She became the mother of his second son, Ferdinand. Meanwhile, Columbus sent his brother to try to interest King Henry VII of England in the great voyage. But Henry thought the idea was madness.

In despair, Columbus decided to try France. But then his luck changed. Ferdinand and Isabella won their war with the Moors. Now they had time to think of other things. Isabella said she was ready to pawn her jewels to help pay for the great voyage—but this was not necessary.

In spring, 1492, Ferdinand and Isabella signed an agreement with Columbus. He was made an Admiral—and would govern any new lands he might discover. He would also receive one tenth of all precious metals in these lands!

Three ships—the Nina, the Pinta, and the Santa Maria—were fitted out in the port of Palos, Spain.

Ninety men were hired as crews. The ships were loaded with supplies and trade goods for the natives they expected to meet.

Then, on August 3, 1492, Columbus set sail on what was to be one of the most important voyages in the history of the world.

Three days out of Palos, the Pinta was damaged. Columbus stopped at Teneriffe in the Canary Islands for repairs. The news came that the King of Portugal was sending ships to arrest Columbus and prevent Spain from exploring the western sea. But Columbus escaped and sailed west.

The trade winds carried the ships

toward the unknown. Each day, when Columbus noted the distance they had gone, he told his men they had gone less. He did not want them to be frightened by the long distance they were traveling. The weather was good and the wind fair. Seven days out of the Canaries, they saw a fiery meteor. This made the crew nervous. Then they came to a great mass of seaweed—and the men were afraid.

They did not think they would fall over the edge of the world. But they did fear hitting rocks amid the seaweed. They did not know they sailed through the Sargasso Sea—a great mass of floating plants that are gathered together by mid-ocean currents.

Columbus made jokes and tried

to cheer the men up. He showed them birds and said that they must be near land. But the crew kept on grumbling.

Another week passed. The trade wind carried them ever westward and some men wondered how they would ever be able to sail back to Europe.

But Columbus knew that the world had "belts" of wind. The trade wind would take them west. To go east, they would strike northward until they entered a wind belt that blew back toward Spain.

More days went by. Still they traveled westward, over an eerie, peaceful sea.

On October 3, the men wanted to change course and follow the sea birds southward. They felt islands lay in that direction. But Columbus insisted they go west, toward the Indies and the riches he dreamed of.

By October 10, the men were near mutiny. No crew had ever sailed so far in one direction without seeing land. They agreed to go on for only three more days. Then they would have to give up and change course.

On October 11, a small branch of a rose bush floated past. Columbus cried: "Thanks be to God! We are near land at last!"

That night, they spotted a light. When the moon rose, they could see limestone cliffs glimmering on the horizon. They could hardly wait for sunrise.

The next day, October 12, 1492, the three little ships anchored off the island of San Salvador in the Bahamas—less than one day's sailing from the coast of Florida!

Solemnly, Columbus took possession of the island in the name of the King and Queen of Spain. A religious man, he prayed that the people of the New World would be-

come Christians. He called the natives "Indians."

They spent the following weeks
sailing the Caribbean Sea, searching
for China or Japan. Columbus felt
sure those countries were someplace
nearby. They discovered Cuba,

which Columbus named *Juana* in honor of the Spanish princess.

And they looked for gold. The Indians had a little, which they traded for beads, bells, and cloth. Then, on Christmas Day, the Santa Maria was wrecked off the coast of Hispaniola. Columbus thought Hispaniola was Japan. No one was hurt in the shipwreck, but the men all saw it as a signal that they should return to Spain. They left 39 men behind in a colony called La Navidad.

Columbus was greeted as a great hero upon returning to Spain. He surprised Ferdinand and Isabella with gold, parrots, and a number of Indians he had brought back with him. Then he made great plans to return to the New World—or the "Indies," as Columbus called the lands he'd discovered.

In September, 1493, he set out with more than 1,200 men in 17 ships to establish colonies in the Indies. The settlement at La Navidad was empty; its men had been killed by Indians. A new colony, which Columbus named *Isabella*, was established nearby. It became the first permanent settlement of Europeans in the New World!

Columbus and his men exlored much of the Caribbean. They made many important discoveries, including the islands of Dominica, Guadalupe, Antigua and Puerto Rico.

But the great navigator proved to be an inefficient governor. His colonies floundered and other men had to be called in to rule them.

Columbus made two more voyages of exploration before Queen Isabella died in 1504. The Admiral's own health failed, and he tried in vain to make the King restore him as Governor of the West Indies. He died, sad and disappointed, in 1506. But his bold ideas and discoveries had changed the course of modern history.

WE THE PEOPLE SERIES

WOMEN OF AMERICA

CLARA BARTON
JANE ADDAMS
ELIZABETH BLACKWELL
HARRIET TUBMAN
SUSAN B. ANTHONY
DOLLEY MADISON

INDIANS OF AMERICA

GERONIMO
CRAZY HORSE
CHIEF JOSEPH
PONTIAC
SQUANTO
OSCEOLA

FRONTIERSMEN OF AMERICA

DANIEL BOONE
BUFFALO BILL
JIM BRIDGER
FRANCIS MARION
DAVY CROCKETT
KIT CARSON

WAR HEROES OF AMERICA

JOHN PAUL JONES
PAUL REVERE
ROBERT E. LEE
ULYSSES S. GRANT
SAM HOUSTON
LAFAYETTE

EXPLORERS OF AMERICA

COLUMBUS
LEIF ERICSON
DeSOTO
LEWIS AND CLARK
CHAMPLAIN
CORONADO